GREAT HOMES OF CALIFORNIA

Text
Bill Harris

Photography
Ric Pattison

Design
Clive Dorman

Editorial
Gill Waugh
Pauline Graham

Production
Ruth Arthur
David Proffit
Sally Connolly

Director of Production
Gerald Hughes

Director of Publishing
David Gibbon

ACKNOWLEDGMENT
The publisher wishes to thank all the individuals and
organizations who so willingly provided assistance, as
well as access to properties, throughout the
preparation and photography for this book. Special
thanks are due to the owners and keepers of the
featured homes, and in particular to the Department of
Parks and Recreation, San Simeon Region, and to the
Meux Home Museum for providing transparencies.

GREAT HOMES OF CALIFORNIA

Text by
BILL HARRIS

CRESCENT BOOKS
NEW YORK

If California were ever to be ruled by a queen, her name would almost certainly have to be Anne. The Golden State is famous for Spanish Mission-style architecture and bungalows that neatly combine indoors and outdoors – nor is it without its Gothic castles and Beaux Arts palaces; but the style that said it all for the Californian Establishment in the late nineteenth century was named for England's Queen Anne and – though the people of the era itself gave credit for its style to Queen Victoria – in California, at least, Anne was clearly the reigning monarch. There is hardly an established community in the state that does not contain at least one ornate, imaginative, Queen Anne-style house.

Actually, the eclectic style we usually call Victorian did not have much to do with that queen of England. However, she was at least aware of it and even appeared to like it. Queen Anne, on the other hand, had been dead for a hundred years before architects started giving her name to their work and, though she probably would have felt familiar with the little details they borrowed from Sir Christopher Wren, she may have wondered about the Dutch details, and she may even have been insulted by the French pretensions of many Queen Anne buildings.

As with so many of the architectural styles Americans have taken to their hearts, the Queen Anne style came to America from abroad. Of course, it became something very different in American hands, and who knows what further American developments would have occurred if the English middle class had not begun demanding new statements of their own in the middle of the nineteenth century.

At the beginning of the century, "People Who Mattered" were building or commissioning Gothic buildings, and it was considered to be quite the height of fashion to live in a house that could double as a church. However, Gothic buildings tended to be dark and drafty, cumbersome-looking and perhaps just a little depressing. Eventually the growing middle class and the younger generation, as younger generations usually do, began rejecting Gothic trappings and demanded something lighter and airier.

This was not the first time the English had engaged in such debate, of course. A century earlier, for example, the "Young Turks" among them looked down their noses at the Italianate villas and town houses of the Georgian élite. They argued that the homes of the upper classes had become so ornate that they were downright vulgar. The real spirit of England, they said, was represented by the country homes of down-to-earth honest yeomen and the work of Sir Christopher Wren.

Architects had reverted to taking tours of Europe in quest of inspiration. However, the new radicals of the mid-nineteenth century believed that, while the Continent may have some ideas to contribute, the best the world had to offer was just around the corner. They still took an occasional look in the direction of Moorish-influenced Spain and the glory that was Greece, and often exhibited a fascination with Japanese art, but when they compared the furniture and buildings of seventeenth-century England to French Gothic and French Rococo, they found their neighbors across the Channel wanting. As one of the early designers pointed out, "Everything English ... is essentially small, and of a homely farmhouse kind of poetry. ... Above all things, nationality is the greatest social trait; English Gothic is small as our landscape is small. It is sweet, picturesque, farmyardish, Japanese, social, domestic. French is aspiring, grand. Straining after the extraordinary is all very well in France, but it is wrong here."

Of course, it was all very well to sit in front of a fire and discuss art, and to exchange letters about what absolutely, positively ought to be done to get a little "Englishness" back into English houses, but it took some effort to realize their ambitions. One of the first attempts was a London house designed by Philip Webb, one of the pioneers of neo-Queen Anne, in 1870. It had enough Gothic arches and gables to make it a good neighbor to the other houses on Palace Green, but it also featured brick moldings and wrought-iron balconies with many other details that had gone out of style in the seventeenth century. The land on which the house was to be built was the property of the Crown,

and therefore plans for construction needed the approval of the Royal Architect before they could begin construction. The Royal Architect came close to throttling the incipient Queen Anne movement at birth by calling Webb's designs not only "hideous," but "commonplace" to boot. Fortunately, Webb's client was well-connected at Court and the Royal Architect's criticism was overruled.

Webb himself could not have been more pleased when his critics were not able to figure out what actual style or period of architecture he had used as the basis for his inspiration. "I take that as a sincere compliment," he said.

Among Webb's characteristic decorations was a sunflower design which, along with a lily motif of his, became all the rage. These appeared – rendered in stone, carved in wood and wrought in iron – over windows, beside doorways and on chimney stacks all over England. The socially conscious had started thinking of the decoration of their houses as something of a duty. As one of them pointed out, "Art is ennobling in itself. It is hellish wickedness to spend more than fifteen pence on a chair when the poor are starving in the street, because you do no good by it. But if you spend five pounds on art in decoration, you do somewhat to elevate your fellow creatures." The movement had begun.

Nonetheless, the Queen Anne style still had a long way to go before it could have any serious claim to being the "in" style of the mid-Victorian era, but it took a giant step forward when J.J. Stevenson, a gentleman architect, built a terrace house in Bayswater as a home for his family and a showcase for his ideas. They were avant-garde ideas in 1871, but not so radical that they could not easily be copied, which indeed they were, in every section of London. Stevenson's Red House was basically the same as hundreds of stucco houses that had been popular in

London for twenty years, but his was faced with brown brick and trimmed with red brick. Anyone with a stucco house could easily reface it that way, and many did. He added Flemish-gabled dormers and leaded glass windows with louvered shutters, which presented no unconquerable challenge to anyone wanting to modernize their house. Without any thought that this was really nothing new but simply aspects of past styles recycled, London began to take on a different look. Though Stevenson and other exponents liked to call what they were doing "Free Classic," their clients much preferred the way the words "Queen Anne" rolled off their tongues. Before long the words "Queen Anne" were on the lips of everyone sincerely interested in showing their neighbors that they knew how to live in style.

It was inevitable that talk of the Queen Anne style should be heard in America too. In the decade after the Civil War, Americans were also beginning to rebel against the Establishment, looking for more sweetness and light than they found among the nouveaux riches and in their already decaying cities. Those who could afford it were rushing off to the seashore or the mountains to escape urban complexity, and what they perceived as simple honesty in the Queen Anne style perfectly matched their mood. However, if American architecture had been nudged toward this style by enthusiastic descriptions of contemporary English houses, it did not need to look to the old country for further inspiration. Anne had been England's Queen when America was England's colony, after all. As a Boston architect pointed out: "To those who believe in revivals, 'Queen Anne' is a very fit importation into our offices. There is no revival so little of an affectation on our soil as that of the beautiful work of our Colonial days. ... It is our legitimate field for imitation, and we have much of it to study right in our own neighborhood."

The American architect H.H. Richardson was the first to take the idea seriously with his Watts-Sherman House at Newport in 1875. Where his English counterparts used tile, he used wooden shingles, where they had used leaded glass, he used wooden mullions, but he retained the tall chimneys and Flemish gables, the wide soffits and the ubiquitous sunflowers of the British version of Queen Anne. However, being proud Americans, Richardson and his former pupils, Charles McKim and Stanford White began a new offshoot of the movement, which they called Colonial Revival. It had an English accent, but it was nonetheless as American as the Declaration of Independence.

The popular Shingle Style that also grew out of the Queen Anne movement was all the rage in the East during the '80s, but it was conceived for the New England climate which produces summers as unbearably hot as the winters are uncomfortably cold. The Queen Anne style was suited to the shady, tree-lined streets of the West, and the style arrived on the architectural scene just as Californians were beginning to see themselves as an established society ready to make a statement of their own. Where the English had built with brick and stone, an abundance of wood in America transformed the Queen Anne style, making it a very flexible vehicle for the imagination. Builders tried to outdo each other with new ways to carve balusters, and designers such as Louis Comfort Tiffany became very wealthy selling the owners of these houses grand stained glass windows, in Tiffany's case, and delicate wrought-iron work. Bay windows were made larger, and towers and turrets more expansive while becoming at the same time more intricate.

Children were treated to the fanciful drawings and illustrations of Kate Greenaway and Randolph Caldecott, perhaps in the hope that their tastes would be turned in a proper direction to reduce the likelihood that they would eventually rise up against the preferred style of their parents. Perhaps this alignment of architecture, art and illustration was one of the reasons why the Queen Anne style survived as long as it did and, even today, many little children live in that happy world where fireplaces are lined with tiles and bay windows glazed with leaded stained glass. Usually the gardens they overlook are the old-fashioned English variety with neatly clipped hedges, a topiary or two and a profusion of colorful flowers. The gardens, too, are a product of the Queen Anne movement.

The Queen Anne style arrived in America with a vengeance at the 1876 Centennial Exposition in Philadelphia, where the British Pavilion consisted of two, half-timbered, stucco manor houses. They appealed to the American desire for a sense of their Colonial history but, more importantly, these houses represented a solution to that elusive search for ways to combine elegance and country charm. The most notable feature of the buildings, and the one Americans took most seriously, was the wide, central entrance hall with its grand staircase and a fireplace to provide a warm welcome. Architects began designing it to be the largest room in their houses and, with the advantages of wood-frame construction and central heating, they were able to make their reception areas still more important-looking by providing large openings into the other rooms. It was a uniquely American development which, a generation later, Frank Lloyd Wright described as an opportunity to eliminate the idea of a room as a box and the house as another. Moreover, where the English had been cautioned that "everything English is essentially small," there was plenty of space on this side of the Atlantic – Americans could let their houses sprawl over the landscape. It meant that the Queen Anne style could take them on real flights of fancy.

Of course, Californians were not without ideas of their own. Apart from the lure of new riches, one of the reasons Easterners went West in the '90s was to escape the old social dogmas that had controlled their lives. They liked the idea of living an informal life, and the climate allowed them to consider new ideas for their houses. While many still looked back to the American East for their inspiration, some adventurous minds looked to the Far East. In this way the bungalow – a word from Hindustani meaning "of Bengal" – arrived on the American scene. Its design was a simple idea, particularly suited to California, of a one-story house with a roof that extended over an open porch. It proved to be an immensely popular style among the new Californians. They could follow plans in magazines or buy them through the mail. Better still, construction was not only simple, it was inexpensive. Of course, it was a style that could also accommodate a grand house, and such architects as Charles and Henry Greene showed Californians how it could be done. The bungalow concept was a way of combining the interior of a house with the outdoors – an idea that not only had an obvious appeal for Californians, but touched a responsive chord from coast to coast. Before long even New Englanders were adding patios to their houses, even though they were unused for more than half the year. The patio, of course, was nothing new. It had been a feature of Californian building long before Paul Revere took his famous nighttime ride around the Massachusetts countryside.

In fact, before the English created Virginia, more than 160,000 Spaniards were already living in North America – more than were living in Spain itself. They had built more than 200 towns, all of them in a Spanish Gothic style that was to endure practically unchanged for 400 years. There were adobe towns all over the Southwest, extending as far north as Kansas before the Franciscans, led by Father Junípero Serra, arrived at San

Diego to build California's first mission in 1769. In the twelve years that followed, Serra, whose missionary work earned him the title Apostle of California, founded eight more Californian missions

His countrymen had for many years been building structures with thick adobe walls and inner courtyards to provide relief from the heat of Mexico and the deserts of the Southwest. Serra followed their example. Of course, he did not go to California to make an architectural statement. The missions and presidios he built were much more primitive than the ones he had seen on his way there. Towards the end of the Spanish period in America, such functional constructions as Serra had built were not developed beyond their original, functional appearance, which was rustic compared to buildings of similar basic style in old Mexico, to which Baroque elements had been added. The result was a plain adobe style that was distinctively "Californian" – similar to, but different from the Spanish Colonial architecture in places like New Mexico. There was little incentive to change or develop this style. It offered a fine combination of indoor and outdoor comfort: good ventilation and thick walls to keep the heat out, and cool patios to make outdoor life a little more bearable. Ironically, as Californian towns began to expand from the original chain of missions, the adobe became anglicized, one of the earliest examples of this form was built by Thomas O. Larkin, whose Monterey house followed the Spanish plan, but included elements of his own that even the Spaniards admired and adopted for themselves.

For all its exotic place names and lingering influence of Spain, California could never have been thought of as an Iberia across the sea. The Spanish had been aware of Alta California since the mid-sixteenth century, but they had their hands full elsewhere and did not see much value in taking the time to explore it, much less settle it. In 1579,

when the Viceroy of New Spain heard rumors that Sir Francis Drake was nosing around, he decided it was time the Spanish did a little exploring themselves. Another seven years passed before the King gave his blessing to the idea, but he did not provide a budget so, two years later, the Viceroy hit on the idea of hiring a free-lance explorer who would be given a share of any riches he might find. A Portuguese Captain, Sebastián Rodríguez Carmeño, rose to the occasion and in return for a Spanish ship and a promise of profit, he sailed away in the direction of Alta California. His ship was caught in a storm and wrecked, but he managed to salvage part of it and limped back to Baja California in a makeshift sailboat. In the process he discovered Drake's Bay and, though he sailed past the Golden Gate to San Francisco Bay, he also sighted Monterey Bay. However, when he arrived back in New Spain nobody was at all happy with him. Not only had he not found any treasure, but he had lost a valuable galleon. All the Spanish had learned from his adventure was not to send any more ships on wild goose chases.

A year later, though, a sharp trader named Sebastián Vizcaíno talked the Viceroy into letting him finance an expedition in return for a monopoly on pearl fishing off the California coast. His first expedition ended in failure when his crew jumped ship, but Vizcaíno was evidently a man who could talk his way out of anything and when he met the angry Viceroy, he tantalized him with tales of a billion pearls just waiting to be taken back to Spain; of salt deposits worth a king's ransom, and of thousands of friendly Indians eagerly waiting to hear the Word of God. Besides, Vizcaíno was again willing to outfit the next expedition himself. All he needed was the Viceroy's permission to do it.

Permission was granted. On November 10, 1602, six months after sailing from Acapulco, Vizcaíno's little fleet of three ships sailed into San Diego Bay. After giving it a name, they sailed north again, discovering and naming the Santa Barbara Islands and exploring the Monterey coast, which he thoughtfully named for the Viceroy. Most of his men were suffering from scurvy by then so he sent them back to Mexico, leaving him with one ship and a decimated crew. He made it as far north as Mendocino before limping back without a single pearl in his hold. The Viceroy was generally pleased, though, and began planning to outfit Vizcaino to establish the first Spanish settlement at Monterey, the name of which, coincidentally, would immortalize his own if California should ever happen to amount to anything.

However, this plan was nipped in the bud. The Viceroy, Count Monte Rey, was promoted to Peru and Vizcaino was made Mayor of a small town in Mexico. The Spanish King, meanwhile, was still intrigued by the idea of colonizing California. The dreams of riches notwithstanding, California represented a base for his fleet of galleons carrying the treasures of the East to Mexico by way of Manila. The King issued a Royal Decree ordering settlement of Alta California. Unfortunately, it was lost in a shipwreck and, by the time it reached Mexico, Vizcaino was on his way home to Spain. Moreover, the new Viceroy had decided to use funds set aside for the colonization of California to finance an expedition seeking islands in the Pacific that would make better relief ports for the treasure ships from the Philippines. By the time they had exhausted their funds and all the possibilities, it seemed that everyone had forgotten about California and no Spanish ship went near it for another 160 years.

During those years, Jesuit missionaries were busily establishing themselves in northwestern Mexico. After the Pope ruled that Indians had souls, the followers of Ignatius Loyola became single-minded

about saving them. As educators, they also civilized the natives, something the old conquistadores had found impossible. As civilized people, the Indians would become tax-paying citizens, which appealed greatly to the Spanish Crown. Better still, the Jesuits were willing to finance their own missions.

However, in the mid-eighteenth century, governments of Catholic countries began to resent the power of the Jesuits and, in 1767, Spain's Charles III ordered their expulsion from his colony of New Spain. The Franciscans, who were already established in some parts of the colony, were ordered to fill the vacuum. By the time Father Junípero Serra arrived on the scene, the Mexican missions were running smoothly and many had been turned over to the regular clergy because the Indians were considered to be thoroughly civilized. But Serra was burning with a passion to convert pagans. He finally got his chance when he accompanied Gaspar de Portolá on an expedition into Alta California in 1769. On July 16 he established a mission at San Diego and began planning what he called a "ladder" of other missions along the coast within a day's journey from each other. By 1823 there would be twenty-three of them extending from San Diego to Sonoma.

Three years later, a group of fifteen grizzly mountain man, led by Jedediah Smith, arrived at the mission at San Gabriel. The priest in charge sent them to San Diego to obtain the Governor's permission to expand their range into California. The Governor not only refused, he also suggested that Smith had better not go near any settlements on his way back East. However, contact had been made and, over subsequent years, more American trappers arrived, willing to risk a Spanish jail for the riches of the Sierra Nevada. Meanwhile, the Russians were extending their sphere of influence downwards from the north, and the Spanish began to realize that their days in Alta California were numbered. Political infighting made it even harder for them to keep their toehold and, by 1844, they had decided that it might be a good idea to be friendlier to the growing number of Americans in their midst. Hard times in the East, beginning in 1837, had convinced hundreds that their only chance to live a worry-free life was to brave the rough trip overland on the Santa Fe Trail. When they got to the end of the trail and discovered the great opportunities to be had, they sent back reports to their less fortunate, former neighbors, encouraging them to follow.

The Mexicans insisted that these migrants apply for citizenship and convert to Catholicism, which sent many off in the direction of Oregon or back over the mountains. However, enough of them accepted the terms and settled to agitate for the annexation of California by the American Government. Such agitation eventually led to war between Mexico and the United States, ultimately winning Washington control of Texas, New Mexico – which at the time included what is now Arizona – and, of course, California. The Americans agreed to pay fifteen million dollars for the territory on May 30, 1848. What no one involved knew at the time was that gold had been discovered four months earlier on the American River at Sutter's Fort, the original site of Fort Ross, which the Spaniards had rudely refused to buy when the Russians had offered it to them seven years earlier for $30,000.

Over the following ten years, California's population grew by some 175 percent. Though most of the newcomers headed for the hills where the gold was, more than twenty percent of the population settled in cities. It was a pattern that had not been seen in America since Colonial times. In the 1850s, less than one percent of the population west of the Alleghenies seemed to prefer an urban way of life. For every

person who was panning for gold there were fifteen Californians involved in what we would call a service industry today, supplying the prospectors with food, clothing, housing, tools of the trade and all manner of fun. It is one reason why, when the gold finally ran out, a surprisingly small number of people ran out on California.

When the gold rush began, farmers in southern California deserted their fields to dig in the mother lode instead. The cattle ranchers who stayed behind were pleased to have new markets for their beef, and spruced up their adobe houses to reflect their new prosperity. It was reported that some of them still had dirt floors, but a great many also contained hand-woven Oriental rugs. Eventually, however, most of the cattlemen were forced off their ranchos through disputes over their Mexican land grants. Sheep farmers took over their rangeland. However, higher prices for grain and produce imported from abroad and from other states eventually lured the farmers back, bringing others to join them. In twenty years, from 1849, the number of farmers in California grew from 1,500 to more than 57,000 and every one of them was turning a nice profit. The gold mines were producing forty-five million dollars a year by 1860, but manufacturing accounted for twenty-three million dollars.

When the gold rush finally ended, California was more like the established states on the East Coast than the old Wild West. Its cities were still growing and the rough and tumble miners moved were replaced by fashionable people with a yen for culture and a taste for the niceties of High Victorian style. Californians had the means to realize such tastes, and they had a feeling for culture themselves. When California was still a Territory, it passed a compulsory education law – something even some fully fledged states on the other side of the Mississippi had not then felt the need for. It was also one of the first states to charter a State

University system, and it established some of the earliest two-year junior colleges anywhere in America. The climate had encouraged writers to make California their home, and the beauty of the place made it the dream home of many artists. It was possible to spend an evening out at the theater or a night at the opera in the California of the 1850s; and the restaurants, not only in San Francisco where they had an almost legendary reputation, but in cities from Sacramento to Los Angeles, contributed to a social scene that could have been the envy of the Eastern Establishment.

It was, of course, at-home socializing that the Victorians treasured most and, as the pioneer days faded from their memories, the second generation of California's first families set out to make a statement for themselves and to prove to non-believers that the Golden State was no cultural backwater.

Enough of them had the means to match their desire to turn California into a showcase of fashionable Queen Anne houses. They could afford to lavish them with rare woods and fabrics, artfully painted glass, intricately carved marble fireplaces, and furnishings in the height of fashion. Like the suddenly rich rancheros of the gold rush years, they imported Oriental rugs almost faster than the weavers could produce them. They had already perceived that California was a veritable Eden, and they added to the beauty around them with gardens to complement their mansions.

By the end of the nineteenth century, San Francisco contained more wood-frame mansions than any other city in the United States. Wood was plentiful, of course, especially redwood, but with so many people using it, there was a trend toward painting it to look like stone or marble. Nobody was fooled, but perhaps one of the key considerations in building a mansion was to make it different from, if not better than, its neighbors by imaginative ornamentation, curiously-turned spindles, intricately jigsawed screens, fancy wrought-iron finials on mansard roofs and domes. A bucket of paint could give a wooden house the look of a marble palace, and Californians in great numbers subscribed to the fashion of painting their houses in a riot of pastel colors. This was not a Californian idea. Even the Eiffel Tower was pink and blue when it was new in 1899. In Californian sunshine, the colors were a wonder to behold. There were no hard and fast rules, though one magazine published in California in the '90s suggested that the facade of Stick Style house looked best when painted maroon, then it went on to recommend: "trimmings, seal brown; sash, ash yellow; roof, dark brown; base, dark Indian red; doors and vestibules, oak." As an alternative it suggested Pompeian red for the base, olive green for the facade, the green of weathered copper for the trim and a Venetian red roof. In San Francisco, especially, homeowners took these suggestions very seriously and added creative touches of their own. As the *San Francisco Chronicle* pointed out when the fashion was at its height, "one is forced to admit that the town does look better for it."

Fashions change of course, and later generations of San Franciscans considered the riot of color to be somewhat garish, if not frivolous, and repainted most of them in shades of dull gray.

During the 1960s, when so many things changed, young people wanting to influence the future looked back to the past and found a means of self-expression in reverting the old houses to something resembling their original appearance. Some say they went too far, others claim they did not go far enough. However, today there are some 16,000 Victorian houses in rows, banking the streets of San Francisco with color and, as fast as the colors fade, it seems, people are out with paintbrushes in their hands and a new color scheme in their heads. Whatever they do, of course, it is really nothing new. Back in 1885, an architectural critic was wringing his hands about "would-be architects" who were finishing their houses "with a bountiful supply of paint, using more colors by far than the tailor who designed Joseph's coat. Red, yellow, chocolate, orange, everything that is loud is in fashion, and the entire exterior is so gay that a Virginia creeper or a wisteria would be bold, indeed, if it dare to set leaf or tendril there."

In spite of his carping, the resurgence of the Queen Anne style may be one of the best things that has happened to San Francisco in our lifetime. Moreover, arguably, the best thing that has happened to California in our generation is the strong urge to recapture and restore the past in preserving the stately old houses and gardens up and down the state. They were built and furnished to make a statement and, thanks to thousands of people with a sense of history, the statement is still being made in impressive Queen Anne mansions, Eastlake row houses, Colonial adobes and even remarkable houses of this century. Many of the furnishings have been lovingly returned to rooms that were designed for them. The gardens have been tended, the glass polished, the woodwork buffed and no history lesson was ever quite as inviting and fascinating as the one to be learnt in these homes where the ghosts of a wonderful past are speaking to anyone who takes the time to listen.

Visitor's Guide

Many of the homes pictured in these pages are open to the public, and some provide guided tours.

Fred Mason House, 1931 T Street, Sacramento. (p.17). Though a private residence, the Mason House is part of a profusion of Victorian mansions in a twenty-square block radius of Sacramento's Old Town, all of which can be seen on a walking tour.

Grand Island Mansion, Box 134, Walnut Grove 95690. (916) 775-1705. (pp. 18-19). The Mansion is available for private parties and special events, and it is open for Sunday brunch from April through mid-December, 10:30a.m.-1:30p.m. Visitors are welcome to browse through the house and grounds. Reservations are required.

Governor's Mansion of California, 16th and H streets, Sacramento 95813. (916) 445-4209. (pp 20-22). Open daily with guided tours. Admission charged.

Vikingsholm, Emerald Bay State Park, Tahoma 95733. (916) 541-3030 (summer only). (pp 23-24). Open daily, July 1 to Labor Day with guided tours. Admission charged. The Park, covering six miles of Lake Tahoe's shoreline, includes nearly 300 campsites. Vikingsholm is reached by foot about a mile from the Emerald Bay Overlook.

Kelley House Museum, 45007 Albion Street, Box 922 Mendocino 95460. (707) 937-5791. (p. 25). Open Friday through Monday, 1p.m.-4p.m. The house is headquarters of Mendocino Historical Research which offers walking tours of other historic houses and buildings in the area.

Bidwell Mansion, 525 The Esplanade, Chico 95926. (916) 895-6144. (pp. 26-28). Open daily 10a.m.-5p.m. with guided tours.

Vallejo Home, Sonoma State Historic Park, Box 167, Sonoma 95476. (707) 996-1744. (pp. 29-30). Open daily.

House of Happy Walls - the Jack London Home, 2400 London Ranch Road, Glen Ellen 95442. (707) 938-5216. (p. 31). Open daily 10a.m.-5p.m. The 1,400-acre State Park that surrounds it opens at 8a.m.

Sam Brannan Cottage and Sharpsteen Museum, 1311 Washington Street, Calistoga 94515. (707) 942-5911. (pp 32-33). Open noon-4p.m. in winter months and from 10a.m. in summer. Group tours available.

Luther Burbank Home and Gardens, Santa Rosa and Sonoma avenues, Santa Rosa 95402. (707) 576-5115. (pp. 34-35). Open Wednesday through Sunday, April though October, 10a.m.-3:30p.m. with a special Holiday Open House during the first weekend in December. Group tours available. Admission charged.

Petaluma Adobe, 3325 Adobe Road, Petaluma 94952. (707) 996-1744. (pp 36-37). Open daily. It is also the site of an annual fiesta on the second Sunday in August.

John Muir National Historic Site, 4202 Alhambra Avenue, Martinez 954553. (415) 228-8860. (p. 38). Open daily 8:30a.m.-4:30p.m., March through August; from 10a.m. September through February.

Shadelands Ranch, 2660 Ygnacio Valley Road, Walnut Creek 94598. (415) 935-7871. (p. 39). Open Wednesdays 11:30a.m.-4p.m.; Sundays from 1p.m. Admission charged.

Camron-Stanford House, 1418 Lakeside Drive, Oakland 94612. (415) 836-1976. (p. 40). Guided tours are given Wednesdays 11a.m.-4p.m. and Sundays 1p.m.-5p.m.

Dunsmuir House and Gardens, 2960 Peralta Oaks Court, Oakland 94605. (415) 562-0328. (pp. 41-43). Guided tours are given Sundays at 1p.m., 2p.m. and 3p.m. April through September. The grounds and gift shop are open noon to 4p.m. Special festivals are presented on Mother's Day, Independence Day and from the week after Thanksgiving until the week before Christmas.

The Lyford House and Richardson Bay Audubon Center, 376 Greenwood Beach Road, Tiburon 94920. (415) 388-2524. (pp. 44-45). Guided tours are given Sundays 1p.m.-4p.m.

The McConaghy Home, 18701 Hesperian Boulevard, Hayward 94544. (415) 581-0223. (pp. 46-48). Guided tours are given Thursday through Sunday 1p.m.-4p.m. The house is decorated for "Christmas 1886" during December.

The G.W. Patterson House and Ardenwood Historic Farm, 34600 Ardenwood Boulevard, Fremont 94555. (415) 796-0663. (pp. 49-51). Open Thursday through Sunday 10a.m.-5p.m., April through November and in December for Christmas tours. The admission charge includes haywagon and railway rides and house tours.

The Lathrop House, Redwood City Heritage Association, Box 1273, Redwood City 94064. (pp. 52-53).

Ralston Hall, 1500 Ralston Avenue, Belmont 94002. (415) 593-1601, extension 201. (pp. 57-59). Tours by arrangement only.

The Haas-Lilienthal House, 2007 Franklin Street, San Francisco 94109. (415) 441-3004. (pp. 54-55). Tours are given Wednesday and Sunday afternoons.

The Whittier Mansion, 2090 Jackson Street, Laguna, San Francisco 94109-2896. (415) 567-1848. (p. 56). Tours of the Mansion can be arranged by contacting the event manager, and the Mansion may also be leased for large-scale entertainments.

Filoli, Canada Road, Woodside 94062. (415) 364-2880. (pp. 60-63). House and Garden tours by reservation only Tuesday through Saturday, February through November. Admission charged.

Winchester Mystery House, 525 S. Winchester Boulevard, San Jose 95128. (408) 247-2000. (pp. 64-67). Guided tours are given daily. Admission charge includes the Mansion, Victorian Gardens and Historical Museum.

Villa Montalvo, 15400 Montalvo Road, Box 158, Saratoga 95070. (408) 741-3421. (pp. 68-70). The Arboretum is open 8a.m.-5p.m. on weekdays; Sundays from 9a.m. The Gallery is open Thursdays and Fridays 1p.m.-4p.m.; Saturdays and Sundays from 11a.m. Admission charged. Group tours by appointment. Call or write for schedules of events.

Plaza Hall, San Bautista State Historic Park, Box 1110, San Juan Bautista 95045. (408) 623-4881. (pp. 71-73). The Park, which is open daily, includes the Mission, the Hotel and other historic buildings.

Casa Amesti, 516 Polk Street, Box 805, Monterey 93940. (408) 372-2608. (pp. 74-77). Open Saturdays and Sundays, 2p.m.-4p.m. Admission charged.

Monterey State Historic Park, 210 Oliver Street, Monterey 93940. (408) 649-2836. (pp. 78-89). Open daily. Admission charge includes tours of historic houses and buildings including the Cooper-Molera Adobe, the Larkin House, Casa Soberanes and the Stevenson House.

Tor House, Box 1887, Carmel 93921. (408) 624-1813. (pp. 90-91). Tours are given Fridays and Saturdays by appointment only.

Meux Home, Tulare and R streets, Box 70, Fresno 93707. (209) 233-8007. (pp. 92-93). Guided tours are given Fridays through Sundays, noon-3:30p.m.

Kearney Mansion, Kearney Park, Fresno 93706. (209) 441-0862. (pp. 94-95). Tours are given Friday through Sunday, 1p.m.-4p.m. Admission charged.

Hearst San Simeon State Historical Monument, Highway 1, San Simeon 93452. (800) 952-5580 in California; (805) 927-4621 in all other states. (pp. 96-102). Access is by one of four different guided tours only. Reservations are recommended. Tours daily every hour from 8:20a.m.-3p.m. in winter and more frequently in summer. Admission charged.

Fernald House, 414 West Montecito Street, Santa Barbara 93101. (805) 966-1601. (pp. 104-105). Open Sunday 2p.m.-4p.m. Admission charged.

Stow House, 304 Los Varneros Road, Goleta 93017. (805) 964-4407. (pp. 106-107). Open Saturdays and Sundays, 2p.m.-4p.m., Memorial Day through Labor Day; Sundays only in other months. Special events include a Fiddler's Convention on the second Sunday in October.

General Phineas Banning Residence Museum, 401 East M Street, box 397, Wilmington 90748. (213) 548-7777. (pp. 108-109). Tours are given Tuesdays, Wednesdays, Thursdays, Saturdays and Sundays at 12:30p.m., 1:30p.m. and 2:30p.m. Donations are requested.

William S. Hart County Park, 24151 San Fernando Road, Newhall 91321. (805) 254-4584. (pp. 110-111). Tours are given Wednesday through Friday 10a.m.-12:30 p.m., and on weekends 11a.m.-3:30p.m. The Park also includes a nineteenth-century railway station and museum.

Dominguez Adobe, 18127 S. Alameda Street, Compton 90220. (213) 636-5981. (pp. 112-114). Open Tuesdays and Wednesdays, and the second and third Sundays of each month, 1p.m.-4p.m. Group tours available.

Los Angeles State and County Arboretum, Queen Anne Cottage, 301 North Baldwin Avenue, Arcadia 91006. (818) 446-8251. (pp. 118-121). Open daily 9a.m.-4:30p.m. Admission charged.

The Fenyes Mansion, 470 West Walnut Street, Pasadena 91103. (213) 577-1660. (pp. 122-127). Open Tuesdays and Thursdays and on the last Sunday of each month for guided tours only. Donations requested.

The Gamble House, 4 Westmoreland Place, Pasadena 91103-3593. (213) 681-6427. (pp. 128-131). Guided tours are given Thursday through Sunday, noon-3p.m. Admission charged.

Tournament House, 391 South Orange Grove Boulevard, Pasadena 91105. (213) 449-4100. (p. 132). Open Wednesdays 2p.m.-4p.m., February through September. Gardens open daily.

The Morey Mansion, 190 Terracina Boulevard, Redlands 92373. (714) 793-2957. (pp. 133-135). Open 1p.m.-5p.m. on the first Sunday of every month. Admission charged.

Kimberly Crest House and Gardens, 1325 Prospect Drive, Redlands 92373. (714) 792-2111. (pp. 136-137). Tours given Sundays and Thursdays 1p.m.-4p.m. Donation requested.

Heritage House, 8193 Magnolia Avenue, Riverside 92501. (714) 782-5273. (pp. 138-140). Open Tuesdays and Thursdays, noon-2:30p.m. and Sundays until 3:30p.m., except during July and August.

Casa de Rancho Cucamonga, Vineyard and Hemlock, Box 401, Rancho Cucamonga 91730. (714) 989-4970. (pp. 141-143). Open Wednesday through Sunday, noon-4p.m. Tours are available.

Scotty's Castle, Grapevine Canyon, Death Valley National Monument 92328. (714) 786-2331. (pp. 144-149). Guided tours are given 9a.m.-5p.m. daily. Admission charged.

The Thomas Whaley House, 2482 San Diego Avenue, San Diego 92110. (619) 298-2482. (pp. 150-151). Open daily 10a.m.-4:30p.m. Admission charged.

Villa Montezuma Museum, 1025 K Street, San Diego 92102. (619) 239-2211. (pp. 152-155). Open Wednesday through Sunday 1p.m.-4:30p.m. Admission charged.

La Casa de Estudillo, Old Town San Diego State Historic Park, 4002 Wallace Avenue, San Diego 92110. (619) 237-6770. (pp. 156-160) Open daily 10a.m.-5p.m. The twelve-acre Park contains sixteen historic structures, seven restaurants and thirty-two retail shops.

The Fred Mason House (facing page) is one of many Victorian style buildings to be found along the streets of Sacramento.

Fifty-eight-room Grand Island Mansion (these pages) was built in 1917 near Walnut Grove by the eccentric German financier Louis Meyers. During the Prohibition years, this house, which is not easily accessible, gained a reputation for being the venue of many illicit parties. Its second-floor entrance hall (facing page bottom) and its bedrooms (below left and bottom) have been restored to look much as they would have done when such people as Earle Stanley Gardner and Jean Harlow were guests at this hideaway.

California's first Governor's Mansion (these pages) was built in Sacramento in 1877 for Albert Gallatin and housed the state's chief executives from 1903 to 1967. Its elegant Victorian entrance hall (above) sets the tone, which is continued into the formal, or first, parlor (above right). At one point during the Mansion's history, the dining room woodwork was painted gray, including that surrounding the mirror over its Italian fireplace (below left). The piano in the music room (below) has been played by such visitors as Liberace. This mansion was not to the taste of Governor Ronald Reagan, who had a ranch-style residence constructed nearby.

The decor of the Blue Room (left) in the California Governor's Mansion (this page), Sacramento, is as it was during the tenancy of Governor Edmund G. "Pat" Brown. The dress suit on the bed belonged to Governor Merriam, whose granddaughter's picture stands on the desk; Governor William Stephen used this room as a nursery for his granddaughter. The French Provincial-style furniture in the guest bedroom (below) was chosen by Mrs. Hiram Johnson in 1911, but the room is maintained as it was decorated by Mrs. Goodwin Knight. The dress on display belonged to Mrs. C.C. Young. Vikingsholm (facing page) on Lake Tahoe's Emerald Bay was built as a summer home for Mrs. Lora J. Knight in 1929. Though not Scandinavian herself, she admired Nordic architecture and commissioned Lennart Palme to build a Swedish home which would do justice to the fjord-like location of Emerald Bay. Sod roofs (facing page top) on the north and south wings were originally covered with wildflowers as well as grass. The dragon suspended from the living room ceiling (facing page bottom) was modeled on beams which hung in old Viking castles to mark areas reserved for the chieftain and his honored guests. There is also a traditional, Swedish bridal table in the living room, brightly painted with a design which incorporates the couple's initials and the date of their wedding.

Much of the furniture in Vikingsholm (this page), including that of the breakfast room (above left), master bedroom (left) and dining room (below), was based on Scandinavian originals and designed by Lennart Palme, who also designed the house. However, the Danish cupboard in the dining room is original and dates back to 1600. The detailed and unusual fireplaces are also of Palme's design, as are the intricate latches to be found all over the house. In fact, a Viking stronghold would have had latches on the outside of every door so that, when the chieftain retired to his second-story tower at night, he could lock everyone in – be they servant or guest. Mrs. Knight, who commissioned the house, was more hospitable, having Palme's latches placed on the inside of the doors to ensure the privacy of her guests.

The town of Mendocino (this page) was established around 1852 by lumbermen from New England. The homes they constructed imitated buildings they admired from other countries. The 1861 Kelley House (above) was the home of one of the city's founders, William H. Kelley. It is now the headquarters of Mendocino Historical Research and contains a museum of original furnishings (above right). William Kelley built the 1882 MacCallum House (right) for his daughter Daisy and her fiancé Alexander MacCallum. After Alexander died, in 1908, Daisy had the house moved to its present location. The Elisha W. Blair House (below right) was built in 1888 for Blair by J.D. Johnson. The house was kept in a state of good repair by all its inhabitants and has, therefore, kept its historic exterior intact. It is one among dozens of fine, original Victorian houses that make Mendocino a very special place.

Italianate Bidwell Mansion (these pages) was built for General John Bidwell, one of the founders of Chico and a pioneering agriculturalist and philanthropist. He made the second largest strike of the California Gold Rush on the Feather River, and purchased Rancho del Aroyo Chico, land on the banks of Chico Creek in the upper Sacramento Valley. Then he hired the renowned San Franciscan architect, Henry W. Cleveland, to build him a twenty-six room villa between 1865 and 1868. A large painting of General Bidwell now hangs in the entrance hall (left). Below: the library. Facing page top: (left) the dining room, and (right) the parlor, suitably draped with the American flag. Facing page bottom: (left) the General's office, and (right) the main guest bedroom.

The Alexander Room (left) and master bedroom (below) have been carefully restored, along with the rest of the twenty-six rooms, to reflect Bidwell Mansion (this page) as it was during the days when General John Bidwell and his wife Annie lived there. Bidwell died eighteen years before his younger wife. After Annie's death Bidwell Mansion became a co-educational school, in accordance with the couple's egalitarian principles. The Mansion was the headquarters of Bidwell's sprawling ranch, from which he introduced such crops to California as the casaba melon. These days, the Mansion is the centerpiece of one of the largest city parks in the United States, most of it bequeathed by Annie Bidwell to the town. Lachryma Montis (facing page), the 1852 home of General Mariano Guadalupe Vallejo at Sonoma, is a classic example of the style known as Carpenter Gothic. The General named the house from the Indian *Chiucuyem*, meaning "Crying Mountain" in reference to the free-flowing spring on the land. Vallejo retained the Indian name but translated it into Latin for "mountain tear." Each of the rooms, including the dining room (facing page bottom), had a white marble fireplace. The house was built of brick to keep it warm in winter and cool in summer.

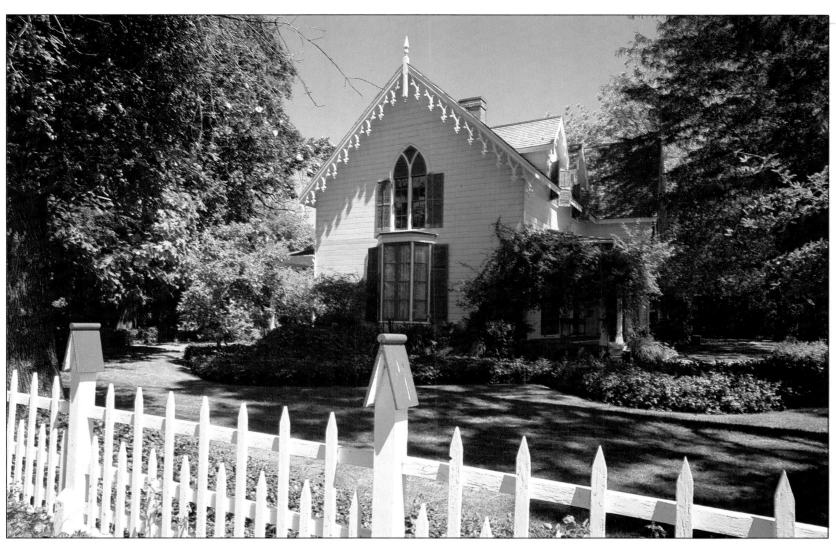

The Gothic arched window in the master bedroom (below) of Lachryma Montis (this page), Sonoma, comes right down to the floor and is among the house's impressive features. The furnishings in the East Bedroom (below), as well as those in most of the other rooms, were selected by Vallejo himself. The rosewood piano in the parlor (bottom) was imported for him from Europe.

To the north of Sonoma and a mile northeast of Glen Ellen stands the House of Happy Walls (this page). It was built in 1922 by Charmian London, widow of writer Jack London, near his beloved Wolf House, which was destroyed by a mysterious fire in 1913 on the night before they were due to move in. Some of London's custom-made furniture, including his roll-top desk and the dictaphone in the study (below), were bought for Wolf House. The Polynesian-inspired dining room (bottom), with a fountain in its floor, was designed especially for Mrs. London.

Sam Brannan, the man who promoted the gold rush in San Francisco and ran California's first newspaper and gristmill, almost created the thriving resort town of Calistoga around natural mineral springs he came across in 1859. Indians called the site *Colaynomo*, meaning "oven place," but Brannan combined California and Saratoga to produce the name Calistoga. His cottage (these pages) was built in 1859, and is now part of the Sharpsteen Museum. Many of the furnishings in the parlor (facing page bottom), its anteroom (bottom) and the bedrooms (below and below left) are original.

Beside the Greek Revival Luther Burbank Home (these pages) in Santa Rosa stands the greenhouse in which he developed some 200 new varieties of plants. Burbank's unmarked grave lies at the foot of a cedar of Lebanon (below). The music room (bottom), dining room (facing page top) and parlor (facing page bottom) saw some illustrious guests: Jack London was a near neighbor and often visited for horticultural tips. Helen Keller, Thomas Edison, Henry Ford and Harvey Firestone were also visitors to Burbank's home.

The Petaluma Adobe (these pages), built in 1834 by General Mariano Guadalupe Vallejo about four miles east of Petaluma, is now the centerpiece of Petaluma Adobe State Park. The Vallejo Suite was the apartment that was home to his family of eleven children. Its rooms, for example the living room (above), dining room (facing page bottom) and bedrooms (below), have been restored to their original state, when they formed part of the grandest residence in California. The Weaving Room (right) contains historical and crafts exhibits, granting a rare glimpse of California during the Mexican period. This huge, two-story adobe house is all that remains of the largest private hacienda in California. It was built as the headquarters of a 64,000-acre land grant, a ranch dedicated mainly to the hide and tallow trade.

The John Muir National Historic Site, at Martinez in the East Bay Area, surrounds the seventeen-room mansion (this page) built in 1882 for John Muir by his father-in-law, John Strentzel, a Polish doctor and revolutionary. The library (above) is paneled entirely in redwood, including the ceiling. The West Parlor (left), in which hangs a portrait of Muir, has a fireplace made of imported onyx. Muir's wife, Louie, was a pianist of concert caliber and would often entertain Muir's conservationist friends with a recital in the parlor. John Muir's study (below left), or "scribble den," where he wrote most of his books and articles, contains his desk, the only piece of original furniture from his years in the house. John Muir was largely responsible for the establishment of Yosemite National Park.

Shadelands Ranch (facing page) is the only historical museum in Walnut Creek, Ygnacio Valley. Eight of its rooms contain furniture belonging to Hiram Penniman, a fruit-farming pioneer, who built the house in the 1850s. Cultivation equipment from the fruit and walnut orchards that once covered the ranch is on display in the museum. It is thought that Hiram built Shadelands for his eldest daughter Mary, whose room (facing page bottom right) can still be seen. He was worried about her future security after his death should she remain unmarried. Facing page: (center left) the dining room, and (bottom left) the parlor.

The Camron-Stanford House (this page) was built in 1876 in Oakland on Lake Merritt. Four of its rooms have been painstakingly restored to their original High Victorian Italianate splendor. Oakland's Dunsmuir House (facing page), built in 1899, is a thirty-seven-room, Colonial Revival mansion.

When Joan Dunsmuir, matriarch of the Scottish-Canadian shipping and coalmining dynasty, gave up control of the family business to her two sons, Alexander Dunsmuir at last felt secure enough to marry. Dunsmuir House (these pages) was built by him as a home for himself and his bride, Mrs. Josephine Wallace, his patient mistress of twenty years standing. Dunsmuir was her wedding gift. Sadly, they never lived together in the house. He died while still on honeymoon and Josephine died in the house only eighteen months later. Facing page: (top) the walnut-paneled formal parlor of the house, furnished in an Edwardian style, and (bottom) the oak-beamed dining room, containing table and chairs which belonged to the Spreckles family. The library (above), with its herringbone-patterned floor, contains furnishings bought by I.W. Hellman Jr. of Wells-Fargo Bank, who purchased the estate in 1906. The bedrooms (right) and master bedroom (below and below right) were also furnished by the Hellmans.

The Victorian home (these pages) of Dr. Benjamin Lyford was moved by barge across Richardson Bay from Marin to Tiburon in 1957. It was refurnished with period pieces and is now the headquarters of the Marin Conservation League and Audubon Society. Beside the house, in its original setting, Lyford set up an experimental "ultra-hygienic" Eagle Dairy. It was situated downwind of the house and was equipped with a chemical septic tank. Lyford strongly advocated cleanliness and the use of a sewerage system in towns, but was only too frequently written off as an eccentric, dirt-obsessed scientist in a time when the importance of good hygiene was barely known. He established a suburban development in Tiburon which he called Lyford Hygeia, a town dedicated to the implementation of his theories of cleanliness and named after Hygeia, the Greek goddess of health. All the furniture in the parlor (below), study (above right), upstairs hallway (above) and dining room (right) has been donated from various sources. Only one couch is thought to be original to the house.

The 1886 McConaghy Estate (these pages), Hayward, a twelve-room Victorian farmhouse maintained with period furnishings, was built by Neil McConaghy – an Irishman who, in 1858, arrived in San Leandro with just five dollars in his pocket. It is seasonally decorated for special holidays such as Christmas and Easter, when eggs are festooned from the dining room chandelier (below). The back porch (right) is kept as if ready and waiting for the servants to come back. Facing page bottom: the front parlor and the hall.

The bedrooms (left, above left and above) at the McConaghy House (this page), Hayward, are maintained as if their occupants were near at hand and soon expected; the table in the children's room (below) is set for an anticipated tea party. The G.W. Patterson House (facing page) in Fremont is part of the 205-acre Ardenwood Historic Farm. Its family parlor (facing page bottom) contains a reed organ dating from 1900, often used to accompany sing-alongs. The house was designed by architect Samuel Newsom, whose firm, run with Joseph Newsom, was an early and prominent proponent of the Queen Anne style during the 1880s and early 1900s. One of the characteristics of this style was the Islamic, or Moorish element, denoting the onion domes, keyhole arches and circular, open kiosks that occurred as either part of a porch or a tower.

The Pattersons' guest bedroom (facing page top and below right), in the George W. Patterson House (these pages), Ardenwood, is lit with rare curved windows and contains a carved Queen Anne bed. Facing page bottom: the guest parlor, with its custom-made stained glass and elegant, rosewood piano. The furnishings in the dining room (above) belonged to the Patterson family. The master bedroom (right) was less elegant than the guest room because it was not used for hospitality, but it was not as Spartan as Nanny's Room (below).

Lathrop House (these pages) was built on Hamilton Street in Redwood City in 1863 for businessman Benjamin G. Lathrop. By October of that year his eleven-room house plus kitchen and servants' quarters was ready for occupation. The Lathrops named the house Lora Mundi, meaning "beauty spot of the world." It is a fine example of Greek Revival building and a rare example of the beginnings of "Steamboat Gothic." The house survived two relocations and the earthquake of 1906. It is now filled with Victoriana and serves as a setting for cultural activities run by the Redwood City Heritage Association. Facing page bottom: the parlor, (above) the den, (right) a collection of Victorian clothing and (below) the Connor family children's room, full of Victorian childhood memorabilia. General Patrick E. Connor, a Civil War hero, bought the house in 1870.

Haas-Lilienthal House (these pages) on Franklin Street is one of the grandest dames of San Francisco's Victorian heritage. A fine example of Eastlake-Queen Anne style, it is resplendent with art-glass windows, various shingles, gables, dormers and a tower accessible only by way of an attic stairway. Its regular bays and incised ornamentation are also examples of the San Francisco Stick Style of the late 1880s. It was built in 1886 for Bavarian merchant William Haas and is now a museum, retaining the original furnishings Haas and the family of his son-in-law, Samuel Lilienthal, collected. Particularly notable are the stencilled leather wall coverings above the paneling in the hallway (bottom). Bottom left: the dining room, (below left) the upstairs sitting room, (below) the bathroom, and (facing page bottom) the Mill Parlor.

The decor of the thirty-one rooms of 1896 Whittier Mansion (this page) on Jackson Street, San Francisco, was arranged with great skill and attention to detail, incorporating handcarved fireplaces, mahogany and white-oak woodwork and rich Oriental rugs. It was built for Franklin Whittier by architect Edward Swain in the Richardsonian Romanesque style, and incorporated electricity when gas lighting was still the norm. Left: the drawing room, (below left) the smoking room, and (above) the reception room. Purchased in 1864 by William Ralston, Ralston Hall (facing page), on the College of Notre Dame Campus in nearby Belmont, was enlarged by his architect John P. Gaynor to become an opulent, eighty-eight-room, Italianate villa. Its ballroom (facing page bottom) is one of the grandest anywhere, recalling the Hall of Mirrors at Versailles.

The past grandeur of Ralston Hall (these pages) is unmistakable in its well-lit gallery (below), set with elegant "opera boxes." Its grand staircase, the airy, mirrored entrance hall (facing page top left), sun porch (facing page top right) and second-floor gallery (facing page bottom) are all as they were when William Chapman Ralston lived there. The estate, originally belonged to Count Leonetto Cipriani. Ralston incorporated Cipriani's modest villa as the core of his creation. In 1922, the Sisters of Notre Dame de Namur purchased the estate as the new site of their college and began the arduous task of restoring the house.

The 650-acre Filoli estate at Woodside includes a forty-three-room mansion (these pages) filled with original furnishings. Willis Polk completed the building for his patron, William Bourn II, in 1916, to a mostly Georgian design, modified by Spanish, Flemish, French and Stuart features. Above left: the imposing, ormolu-embellished fireplace in the ballroom (facing page bottom), and (above and facing page top) the drawing room. Left: the walnut-paneled library with a Sir Thomas Lawrence painting hanging over the fireplace, (below left) the study, and (below) the passage seen from the drawing room. The chandeliers hanging in the ballroom are said to have hung in the Hall of Mirrors in Versailles when the Treaty of Versailles was signed. Six crystal side sconces, hung with amethyst drops, further illuminate the room. The estate was named using a form of acronym of Bourn's motto: "FIght, LOve, LIve" – fight for a just cause, love your fellow man, live a good life.

A bell in the imitation Christopher-Wren-design cupola surmounting Filoli's Carriage House (facing page) rings every half-hour and can be heard on a prevailing breeze throughout the gardens (these pages). Filoli's Italian Renaissance Tea House (facing page bottom) was designed by Arthur Brown, Jr., a prominent San Franciscan architect, who also designed the Carriage House. The Filoli estate reminded William Bowers Bourn, for whom the house was built, of County Kerry and Killarney, Ireland, where he had bought Muckross House. He imported many of the garden's yew trees, yew hedges and holly trees from Muckross. His time in England at Cambridge University had instilled in him an admiration for the architecture of the British Isles as well, and this influenced considerably his choice of style for Filoli House (above).

Winchester House (these pages), in San Jose, is the 160-room Victorian mansion of Sarah Winchester and is the result of thirty-eight years of continuous construction. It contains a museum of guns, particularly of the Winchester rifle (below) – the "Gun That Won the West" and made Sarah Winchester's fortune. The house contains such oddities as doors that lead nowhere, a chimney that rises four floors to stop one and a half feet from the ceiling, and stairs terminating in the ceiling. Obsessed with guilt at the deaths caused by the gun which provided her inheritance, and convinced that the deaths of her daughter and husband, the Winchester heir, had been brought about by the vengeance of the dead, she consulted a spiritualist who told her that if she funded permanent construction she would not die. Construction lasted from 1884 until her death in 1922, aged eighty-two.

For all its eccentricities, the Winchester Mystery House (these pages) is a treasure-trove of Victoriana, a fine example of which is the Tiffany window (below right) at the top of the main staircase. The ballroom (facing page top) contains a pipe organ and is lit by a chandelier with thirteen candles. Sarah Winchester had a strong belief in the occult power of the number thirteen. Even her will contained thirteen distinct parts and she signed it thirteen times. The house contains forty-seven fireplaces, as well as a central heating and a sprinkler system to protect it from fire. Above left: the front parlor, and (above) the sitting room of the hall of fires. Below left: a shady arbor, and (facing page bottom) Mrs. Winchester's bedroom.

The Mediterranean-style Villa Montalvo (these pages) was built in 1912 by James Duval Phelan, a former mayor of San Francisco and California's first popularly elected U.S. Senator. It lies at the feet of the Santa Cruz Mountains near San Jose. The solarium (facing page) is a perfect expression of the sun-drenched Californian lifestyle. The villa was named for the sixteenth-century Spanish writer, Garcia Ordoñez de Montalvo. One of his fictional characters, an Amazonian queen named Califia, ruled an island rich with jewels and gold, and he called the island California, a land "close to the Terrestrial Paradise." It is hardly surprising that, on first sighting the Golden State, Spanish explorers named it after Montalvo's mythical land. Senator Phelan filled the house with artist friends, and today Montalvo is a center for the arts.

Villa Montalvo (this page) now provides the setting for a variety of concerts, exhibitions, poetry readings, plays and dance performances. The 175-acre estate also contains an arboretum and a bird sanctuary. Below: the library, and (bottom) the main hall of Montalvo. Plaza Hall (facing page), also known as the Zanetta House, in San Juan Bautista State Historic Park, was built in the 1860s by Angelo Zanetta, who hoped it would serve as the San Benito county courthouse. Instead it became his residence, with a dance floor upstairs noted for its spring. Facing page bottom: the kitchen.

Plaza Hall (these pages), facing San Juan Plaza, was acquired by Angelo Zanetta in 1868. The original adobe building on the site had once quartered the Spanish cavalrymen of General José Castro. Earlier than that it had probably been a *monjerio*, a dormitory for unmarried mission Indian women. Zanetta modified it to be his family residence and furnished it in mid-century splendor. Facing page: (top) the main parlor, and (bottom) the back parlor. Right: the study, and (below) a family bedroom.

Casa Amesti (these pages), in Monterey, now the Old Capital Club, is a charming example of California Colonial architecture, influenced by the work of architect Thomas O. Larkin. It was built between 1834 and 1853 by José Galo Amesti, but it was later transformed by the noted interior designer Frances Elkins, who bought and restored the house in 1918. It is one of the earliest Californian homes to show the influence of Southern plantations during the period before the Mexican War and the United States' acquisition of California. The library (above) contains an antique bookcase, still coated in its original paint, that was taken from a French château. Facing page bottom: the living room, or *sala*, spread with rare Chinese rugs, each woven for the coronation of a Chinese emperor. Below: a bedroom, and (right) the dining room, lit by a French crystal chandelier.

Left: the living room of Casa Amesti (these pages), Monterey. The Green Lounge (below) was Mrs. Elkins' bedroom. She decorated it in green, black and white and her theme wove around dolphins, stags and sea shells. Hence the sand-dollar chandelier. The upstairs hall (facing page top) is hung with antique wallpaper made in France by Jean Zuber and Company around 1834, the same year in which the house was built. The two corner cupboards, Chinoiserie lacquer encoignures, are lovely examples of eighteenth-century workmanship. The Chinese porcelain jars date from around 1800. From the dining room (facing page bottom), at the back of the house, there is a magnificent view of the gardens, designed by Mrs. Elkins' brother, David Adler, in 1919.

The Cooper-Molera Adobe (these pages) in Monterey is a two-and-a-half acre complex of adobe buildings and period gardens around the town house of Captain John Rogers Cooper, a sea captain and trader who established a ranching empire in California after his arrival in 1823.

The rooms of the Cooper-Molera Adobe
(these pages) are filled with impressive
Victorian antiques, reflecting the opulent
lifestyle of a nineteenth-century family.
Captain Cooper married a local girl,
Encarnacion Vallejo, whose sister was
married to José Amesti and lived across
the street at Casa Amesti. The bride's
brother was the famous General Mariano
Vallejo. Left: the Skylight Room, and
(below) the dining room. Facing page:
(top) the upstairs parlor, and (bottom)
the parlor.

The 1835 Larkin House (these pages), in Monterey, was built by Thomas Oliver Larkin, half-brother of Captain John Rogers Cooper, who owned the Cooper-Molera Adobe. Like other homes in the area, it combined aspects of the Spanish Colonial style with styles popular in New England to create a new form called Monterey Colonial. Larkin's was the first two-storied adobe in California. The wraparound verandahs and low-hipped roofs were his invention. Larkin became a prominent citizen. Being one the very few early immigrants not to take Mexican citizenship, he became the United States' first and only consul to Mexican California. The house is furnished as it was when the Larkin family lived here, containing many items that belonged to Larkin. Facing page bottom and above: the parlor, and (below) the dining room. Right: the room of Mr. Toulmin, a subsequent owner of Larkin House, and (above right) a family bedroom.

The bedrooms in the Larkin House (this page), Monterey, reflect an elegance established by one of early California's most influential men. The master bedroom (below) features a magnificent carved bed and Oriental-style furniture. Bottom: the Rose Room.

Casa Soberanes (this page) in Monterey contains a fine collection of local art mixed with New England-style furnishings. It was built in the 1830s for José Rafael Estrada in the usual Californian style, with three-foot-thick adobe walls and redwood beams. Bottom: the parlor.

Casa Soberanes (this page), Monterey, was restored to its original appearance in the 1920s. Its thick adobe walls make the windows and doors among the house's most interesting features. The thickness of the walls can be very clearly seen by looking at the parlor window (above). Above left: the front door, and (top) a bedroom. The two-story adobe Stevenson House (facing page) was built in the 1830s. It takes its name from the fact that writer Robert Louis Stevenson lived here when it was a rooming house.

The Stevenson House (these pages) has been restored to the time when it was used as a rooming house, and several of its rooms contain mementos of Robert Louis Stevenson, who came to Monterey in 1879 to be near his future wife, Fanny Osbourne. The articles he wrote about Monterey are published in the collection *From Scotland to Silverado*. The house has since become a museum of Stevenson memorabilia and even contains the desk at which he wrote *Treasure Island*. Above: the kitchen, and (above left) the childrens' room. Facing page: (top) the boarding house parlor, (center left) the library, (bottom left) the dining room, and (bottom right) the ladies' bedroom.

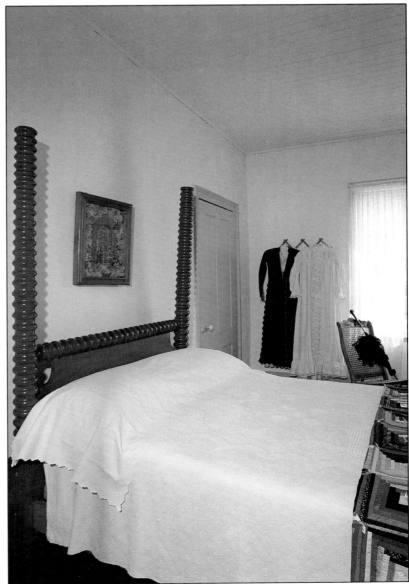

Tor House (these pages), Carmel, is filled with mementos of poet Robinson Jeffers, including his much-loved Steinway piano (facing page bottom). Una's alcove (below) was his wife's workplace. He said of her: "She never saw any of my poems until they were finished and typed, yet by her presence and conversation she has co-authored every one of them." The dining room fireplace (below) stands on the site of an ancient firepit used by Costanoan Indians. In his famous poem, *The Bed By the Window*, Jeffers wrote: "I chose the bed [(bottom)] downstairs by the sea-window for a good death-bed." He died in it in 1962.

The 1889 Meux Home (these pages) in Fresno was built for the former Confederate surgeon and pioneer physician Thomas R. Meux. It is a rare survivor of the dozens of grand Victorian houses built during Fresno's first twenty years. It has been restored and furnished with items that reflect the lifestyle of an upper-middle-class family between 1880 and 1920. The master bedroom (facing page bottom right) and dining room (bottom) are found in the

octagonal-shaped tower. The library (below) contains a photograph of Meux aged twenty-six in his Confederate uniform; there is also a similar uniform on display. Nearly all the books in the library belonged to Thomas Meux. Below left: the parlor, and (facing page bottom left) a child's room, containing a collection of turn-of-the-century toys and dolls.

Martin Theodore Kearney, "The Raisin King of California," built Kearney Mansion (these pages) in 1903 as the Superintendent's Lodge at the heart of his 5,000-acre Fruit Vale Estate in Fresno. Kearney Mansion is built of adobe bricks made on the estate. The house is notable for the French wallpapers Kearney commissioned, and the hand-carved Black Forest oak furniture he bought in Germany. Bottom: Kearney's bedroom, and (below) the hallway. Facing page: (top left) the dining room, (top right) Kearney's office and (bottom) the reception room.

William Randolph Hearst's castle (these pages), San Simeon State Historical Monument, incorporates 123 acres of gardens, terraces and guest houses. The focal point is La Casa Grande, the Moorish-Spanish mansion, begun in 1922. It is a spectacular example of Mediterranean Revival architecture designed by Julia Morgan, Hearst's architect. "The way God would have done it if he had had the money," is how George Bernard Shaw described it after a visit to what the Hearst's called La Cuesta Encantada, or "the enchanted hill." Overleaf: the 103-foot Neptune Pool, a swimming pool graced with Italian and Vermont marble.

The many rooms of Hearst's Casa Grande (these pages) are filled with furniture and antiques collected by Mr. Hearst. The list includes Gothic and Renaissance furniture, sixteenth-century tapestries, Greek pottery, Roman mosaics, medieval paintings and Neoclassical statuary. All of the rooms were designed around their furnishings, and all of the materials used had to be hauled some 1,600 feet to the top of the hill overlooking the Pacific Ocean. Facing page: one of the elaborate twin bell towers, embellished with blue and gold tiles. The towers hold a thirty-six-bell carillon made in Belgium and were patterned after a Spanish cathedral. A Moorish influence is very evident in their architecture.

The refectory (above) was Hearst's favorite room in his San Simeon estate (this page). The silk banners hanging out from the walls represent districts of the Italian city of Siena. The Gothic study (left) was part of his private suite, and guests waited in the Assembly Room (below left) for their host to greet them. The gold tiles of his indoor pool (below) are reflected in Venetian glass. The 1875 Fabing-McKay-Spanne House (facing page) in Lompoc is less imposing, but represents the lifestyle of one of California's early families. It was built for Henry Wadsworth Fabing and its interiors have been furnished with antiques donated by descendants of Lompoc Valley pioneers.

The fourteen-room Fernald House (these pages) in Santa Barbara is filled with mementos of the family of a local judge, Judge Fernald, who occupied it for more than eighty years. The last surviving member of the family, Florence Fernald, gave piano lessons in the music room (facing page bottom) until her death in 1958. The carved staircase, doors and wainscoting were all created by Roswell Forbush, a local cabinet maker. Above: the dining room, and (right) the library.

Stow House (these pages) in Santa Barbara was built in 1873 by Sherman P. Stow as the headquarters of a 1,000-acre ranch that produced almonds and walnuts and on which was raised California's first commercial lemon grove. It became a house museum in 1967 and its rooms were restored according to the decor of the Victorian era, containing appropriate furniture, artifacts and period clothing. The Stow Room (facing page bottom), or study, used to be the master bedroom (below right). Above: the living room, and (right) the dining room.

The Greek Revival Phineas Banning Residence (these pages), in Wilmington, was frequently at the center of Los Angeles social life following its completion in 1864. Its reception room (left) is furnished in the Early Empire style. The parlor (below) contains furniture of laminated rosewood in a style which was an American modification of French Rococo Revival – very popular throughout the 1860s. The mantel over the fireplace in the family living room (facing page top) was handcarved for the house by William Stotzner, a German craftsman specially commissioned to do the work. Stotzner also carved the 1889 Italian Carrara marble statue which stands in the corner between the window and the mantel and is called *Volere e Potere*, or "Where there is a will, there is a way." The unusual American Gothic-style wooden bird cage in the window dates from the mid-nineteenth century. The room is a very good example of what has latterly been called "the Victorian devaluation of space." The girls' bedroom (facing page bottom) contains an ornate bed bought for the Bannings' daughter, Lucy.

The house (these pages) of film star William S. Hart was built at Newhall in 1927 on a former ranch that had been used as a location for some of his Westerns. Hart commissioned Los Angeles architect Arthur Kelly to design a Spanish Colonial house, which he called La Loma de los Vientos, "Hill of the Winds." The home is filled with treasures reflecting his interest in the legacy of the West. Among the guns (left), bison heads, textiles and costumes is a portrait of "Two Gun Bill" by James Montgomery Flagg, which hangs in the dining room (facing page bottom). Above: the living room, and (below) Hart's sister, Mary Ellen Hart's room. Below left: Hart's room. When Hart died, in 1946, he bequeathed his house to the County of Los Angeles. "While I was making pictures, the people gave me their nickels, dimes and quarters. When I am gone, I want them to have my home."

The 1826 Dominguez Ranch Adobe (these pages) at Compton was originally the home of Juan José Dominguez, whose rancho was the first granted in Spanish California and, in 1858, the first to receive a Patent of Title from the United States. Its rooms today, including the chapel (right) and dining room (below), are furnished as they were in Colonial days. Dominguez was a member of the Spanish pioneer expedition that arrived in San Diego on June 29, 1769, having traveled 400 miles overland from the Presidio of Loreto in Baja California. For the next thirteen years his task was to protect Junípero Serra and his fellow Franciscan Padres in their efforts to found a chain of California missions. Appropriately enough, the house was deeded by Dominguez women faced with the problem of no male heir, to the Claretian Order of Missionaries.

Original furniture that belonged to the Dominguez family provides part of the charm of the Dominguez Ranch Adobe (this page) in Compton. The blocks of granite used to build the walls of Frank Lloyd Wright's Ennis-Brown House (facing page), rising over Los Feliz in Los Angeles, were quarried on site. The house clearly shows the profound influence of Mayan Indian temple architecture on his work during the 1920s. Facing page bottom: the dining room.

Uncharacteristically, its architect, Frank Lloyd Wright, did not design the furnishings for the Ennis-Brown House (these pages), in Los Angeles. However, the fireplace in the living room (facing page bottom, below and below right) is surmounted by the only surviving example of the four glass mosaics that Wright designed. The numerous stained glass windows were created by Orlando Giannini to Wright's designs. The Ennis-Brown House was the setting for the '60s movie *The House on Haunted Hill*.

The lakeside Queen Anne Cottage (these pages) was built in Arcadia, Pasadena, in 1886 by Elias Jackson "Lucky" Baldwin for his fourth wife, sixteen year old Lillie Bennett, whose father, architect Albert A. Bennett, designed the house. For many years it was thought that Baldwin had built it for Jennie Dexter, his third wife, who died in 1881 and whose portrait in stained glass graces the Cottage's front door. It is a combination of popular Victorian styles: Queen Anne mixed with Eastlake and Stick style. The gaming table in the parlor (below) is lit by a pair of exquisite stained glass windows.

The walnut secretary (above) in the study of the Queen Anne Cottage (these pages), Arcadia, contains a set of nineteenth-century encyclopedias. Hanging over the study mantel is a portrait of hotel man "Lucky" Baldwin, who had the Cottage built. The chandelier (below right) in the parlor (above right) is a Viennese design in crystal, illuminating an oil portrait of Jennie Dexter, Baldwin's third wife, which hangs by the fireplace. Jennie died aged twenty-three, probably of tuberculosis. The house became a shrine to her after Baldwins' fourth wife, for whom he built the house, left him before it was completed. The bedroom furnishings (below left) are made of burled walnut in the Eastlake style. The bathroom (facing page) contains a zinc-lined tub to prevent corrosion, and redwood paneling.

The Fenyes Mansion (these pages) on Orange Grove Avenue – "Millionaires Row" – in Pasadena was built in 1905, designed by architect Robert Farquhar for Mrs. Eva Scott Fenyes. Her husband, Doctor Adelbert Fenyes, practiced medicine from here. This Beaux Arts building is among the best on the West Coast. On the mantel of the master bedroom (left) stands a rare Willard clock, and it is believed that Ignace Paderewski played the Steinway piano in the parlor (facing page top) when the mansion was used as the Finnish Consulate. Eva's granddaughter, Leonora, married George Paloheimo from Finland who, in 1947, was appointed the first Finnish Consul to the Southwest United States. The foyer (facing page bottom) contains furniture and artifacts from all over the world. Against the wall, between portraits of Rebecca and Leonard Scott, Mrs. Fenyes' parents, and under a gilt mirror, stands a splendid vargueña chest from Spain, which has secret compartments used to hide valuables during the Spanish Inquisition.

The second-floor solarium (below) was a late addition to the Fenyes Mansion (these pages), Pasadena. The solarium is part of an added two-story wing (facing page bottom) designed by Sylvanus Marston in 1911. Unlike many additions to fine old buildings, Marston's work was sensitive to the original structure and architecturally compatible. The main house was designed by Robert Farquhar, who also had a hand in designing the Pentagon in Washington D.C. The children's bedroom (facing page top) contains an American-made four-poster bed and a woven wicker crib.

The office (facing page top) in the Fenyes Mansion (these pages) was originally Dr. Fenyes' bedroom, but was converted to an office during the mansion's days as a Consulate. On the desk stands a lamp signed by Louis Comfort Tiffany. The portrait over the fireplace in the dining room (facing page bottom) is of Mrs. Fenyes, whose father founded the New York Scott Publishing Company. She looks as if she is still sitting at the head of her neo-Renaissance oak dining table. The studio (this page) was added to provide more room for family hobbies and entertaining. Two Beluchistan rugs, one beside the piano, are lovely examples of prayer rugs. In order for the faithful to be pure when praying, it was believed that the space on which they prayed must also be pure. Hence the creation of prayer rugs. Later the rug itself was often endowed with mystical properties, leading to legends of flying carpets.

The David B. Gamble House (these pages) in Pasadena was designed and built in 1908 for the Procter and Gamble heir, David B. Gamble, by Charles Sumner Greene and Henry Mather Greene. It constitutes one of the finest examples of the American Craftsman Movement and one of the finest examples of the California Bungalow style. Its dining room (facing page top) and living room (facing page bottom) contain lighting fixtures of Tiffany glass, all designed, as was the furniture, by the architects. The gardens (bottom) are overlooked by a great bay window.

The entrance hall (facing page top) of the Gamble House (these pages), Pasadena, is lit through a three-panel Tiffany screen creating the luminous effect of a Japanese silk print. The house has five bedrooms, but the Gamble's two sons shared one (facing page bottom) between them. The furnishings in the room (top) used by Mrs. Gamble's aunt were designed for the house, but not by Green and Green. They did, however, create the inlaid black walnut furniture found in the master bedroom (above).

The headquarters of the Pasadena Tournament of Roses Association, Tournament House (this page), was begun in 1906 for the George Stimson family. Before it was finished in 1914 the family had scattered and the Stimsons sold their empty nest to William Wrigley, Jr., the Chicago chewing gum manufacturer. In 1958, the house and its four and a half acres of gardens were donated to the City of Pasadena. These days its elegantly furnished rooms are working spaces for the Association that organizes the famous New Years' Day celebration. Below: the living room, paneled in Circassian walnut, and (below left) the dining room, paneled in figured mahogany and lit by a chandelier of Czechoslovakian crystal. The 1890 Morey Mansion (facing page) in Redlands is a fascinating combination of styles: a Moorish or Saracenic onion-shaped dome, French mansard roof, Chinese tracery verandah, Italianate balustrades and Gothic windows grafted onto a Queen Anne mansion. It was built for the retired ship owner David Morey with money from his wife's tree farm, and his was the inspiration behind the many nautical touches in the house.

The Morey Mansion (these pages), Redlands, was built in 1890 by shipbuilder David Morey, who lavished its twenty rooms with finely carved, golden oak woodwork. It is now a private home, restored to all of its former glory. The reed organ in the dining room (facing page top) was a standard amenity in Victorian homes, but not often used to provide dinner music. The bathroom shower (bottom) was a rarity in the 1890s.

Kimberly Crest (these pages), a Victorian adaptation of a French château, in Redlands, is furnished exactly as it was during the seventy-five years for which it was home to the family of John Alfred Kimberly, a founder of the Kimberly-Clark Corporation. It overlooks the Redlands Valley, affording a splendid view of the San Bernardino Mountains. Its main hall (below left) is overlooked by a Minstrel's Gallery (left). The French Revival parlor (facing page bottom) was designed by the studios of Louis Comfort Tiffany. The photograph on the table is of Mrs. Kimberly. The furnishings in the dining room (facing page top) are Kimberly family heirlooms.

Heritage House (these pages), in Riverside, abounds with touches of early Georgian style, but is in the main a beautiful example of the Queen Anne style. It was built in 1892 for Catherine Bettner, widow of James Bettner, a civil engineer turned orange grower, and is now furnished in high Victorian style and filled with such little treasures as the stereoscope on the table in the music room (below). It was one of the first houses in the area to use gas lighting. Above: the ivory and gold leaf parlor, and (above right) the dining room. Right: the master bedroom.

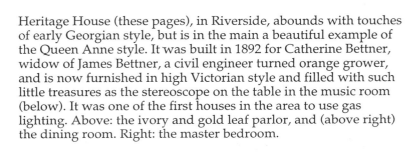

The elaborate oak stairway (below) in Heritage House (this page) leads to a balcony that gives access to the library (left) – a very masculine room for the home of a widow who lived alone. The house was designed by John Walls of the architectural firm of Morgan and Walls. The John and Merced Rains' House at Rancho Cucamonga (facing page) was built in 1860 of bricks made on the site. Mrs. Rains was the daughter of Isaac Williams, a Chino cattle rancher. Her husband was mysteriously murdered a year after moving into the house. She remarried and had four children, added to the five Rains had fathered, which may explain why Cucamonga's first school held classes in her house. She eventually to give up her house after a long legal battle with her brother-in-law, who had been accused of her husband's murder, and was also suspected of murdering her second husband's brother. However, he was never actually convicted and, after he himself was killed in a duel, Merced lost her home in a sheriff's sale and moved to Los Angeles.

The Rains House (these pages), Casa de Rancho Cucamonga, was scheduled for demolition in 1971, but was saved by a junior high school teacher who stood in the path of the bulldozers. Her students followed her in a "March For History" and the building was rescued. The following year, the Rancho Cucamonga Historical Society began a long labor of love, restoring and refurnishing the house in the style of the 1860s. Above: the dining room, and (below) the parlor. Left: the hallway. Facing page: (top) the middle bedroom, and (bottom) the master bedroom. The house is the oldest brick building in the county and lies on the site of a prehistoric Indian settlement.

Scotty's Castle (these pages), Death Valley, was built over a nine-year period by insurance executive Albert Johnson, who named it in honor of Walter E. Scott, a former Wild West Show cowboy and sometime gold prospector whom Johnson had staked. When Scott left the show after a dispute with Buffalo Bill Cody, he took two gold souvenir nuggets that his wife had been given in Colorado, claimed they were from a secret gold mine in Death Valley and went in search of wealthy grubstakers. One of his most long-term stakers was Johnson, a mining engineer with a degree from Cornell University. They were complete opposites: Johnson was a nonsmoking, nondrinking, nonswearing religious man, and Scott spent his entire grubstake on wine, women and song. Left and facing page: the sprawling stucco hacienda's Great Hallway, filled with custom-made leather furniture.

The carved redwood ceiling in the upper music room (facing page) of Scotty's Castle (these pages), Death Valley, provides perfect acoustics for the fifteen-rank Wurlitzer pipe organ. A twenty-five-note keyboard is wired to play the Deagan chimes in the Chimes Tower from the lower music room (below). Bottom: the dining room.

In Scotty's bedroom (facing page top), Scotty's Castle (these pages), Death Valley, a portrait of his former boss, Buffalo Bill, hangs near the door. Furnishings in the other bedrooms include an antique bed from Spain in Mrs. Johnson's room (facing page bottom). The Italian Suite (above) is furnished with pieces from Italy and Spain, including one of fifteen Majorcan rugs found in the Castle. The kitchen (right) is decorated with tiles imported from Spain. An inscription in Spanish, carved in a kitchen beam reads: "Serve yourself to all you desire. Be seated. You are welcome." Even after discovering Scotty's perfidy and losing most of his fortune in the Wall Street Crash of 1929, Johnson still welcomed him to his house. Being led on wild mule chases around Death Valley in Scott's company, ostensibly in quest of his mine investment, had improved Johnson's failing health; and being beguiled by Scott's entertaining stories and more than adequate cooking had endeared the man to him. The nonexistent mine ceased to matter. Even when Scott put it about that the Castle in progress was actually his, funded by the mythical Death Valley gold mine, Johnson humored him – which is the reason why Johnson's home is called Scotty's Castle. Johnson once explained: "Scotty repays me in laughs."

The Whaley House (these pages) in San Diego's Old Town, was built for Thomas Whaley in 1857. It is the oldest brick structure in Southern California. Among its rooms restored to their original appearance is the Court Room (right) where the town's business was transacted and trials conducted in 1869 and 1870. Whaley wrote to his mother: "My wife has every comfort and luxury I can afford to give her … My parlor [(facing page bottom)] is furnished with Brussels carpet and mahogany and rosewood furniture, a mahogany crib for little Frank. We frequently have musical soirées and our house is the resort of most of the best people in the place." Above: the dining room, (below) a bedroom, and (below right) the study.

Villa Montezuma (these pages), a fanciful Queen Anne style mansion in San Diego, was built in 1887 by author and musician Jesse Shepard. It is especially noted for its art glass windows, depicting Sappho, in the music room (facing page top). A motif of grapes and flowers appears in the stained glass windows of the reception room (facing page bottom), which was originally decorated entirely in pink. It has recently been refurnished with Oriental pieces. The woodwork throughout the house is native redwood.

The windows in the conservatory (below) at Villa Montezuma (these pages), San Diego, represent the four seasons. The Red Room, or Shepard's bedroom (facing page top), was originally completely fitted out in red, except for its white walls, which were decorated with gold fleurs-de-lis. In the redwood-paneled drawing room (facing page bottom) hangs a round portrait of Jesse Shepard painted during a visit to Russia. Its bay window is set with art glass portraits of Shakespeare, Goethe and Corneille. The drawing room door leads into the music room.

Casa de Estudillo (these pages) in San Diego's Old Town, built in 1827, has recently been restored and remains a typical one-story adobe townhouse. Its rooms are furnished in the style of the Spanish Colonial period, when it was home to the family of San Diego Presidio, Commandante José María de Estudillo. The twelve-room Casa also has a chapel. Above: *la sala*, the family room, and (facing page bottom) the dining room.

157

When 1827 Casa de Estudillo (these pages and overleaf) was restored in 1908 it was known as "Ramona's Marriage Place," and a garden was planted (overleaf) to provide a setting for outdoor weddings. The bedrooms (this page) and the kitchen (facing page) of Casa de Estudillo are now almost exactly as they were during the century after California's first Spanish mission was established in San Diego by Father Junípero Serra on July 16, 1769, making San Diego "the place where California began."

INDEX